andwhenikissedyou.

(THE THOUGHTS AND POEMS OF A HOPELESS ROMANTIC, LOST IN A HOOKUP CULTURE.)

DVONTE JOHNSON

DVonte Johnson

Copyright © 2018 by DVonte Johnson

Andwhenikissedyou.

This is for the hopeless romantic.

For the one that is so deeply in love, they will die trying to find

it.

For the one that is so sweet, so kind,

so tender, so giving,

so damn special, that nobody will compare too.

This is for the hopeless romantic, that is so lost in the essence

of trying to find love,

they never found themselves because they were so busy trying

to find someone else.

This is for you.

A Message To You:

Why do we fight for something that should be so easy to give to one another? Love is something that is so pure, but yet so many of us are living in this world lonely, sad, and depressed.

We are faced with aspirations of the perfect relation- ship. We are forced to watch movies that show this "fairytale" type of love that is only made for the cinema.

All of us are hopeless romantics, all of us.

We all hope to find love, we all don't want to die alone. But we choose to chase the materialistic side of love, rather than the side that we need the most.

We choose to chase the pretty one, rather than the one that checks up on us everyday.

We choose to chase the one with the most ambitions, only hoping to see how they can benefit us in the future.

We strive on love so long, that we die being the hope- less romantic that we all dream of.

This is the new reality of love, in which we have lost the hopeless romantic.

Pain.

I.

Thank you.

Thank you for rejecting me.

Thank you for telling me that I wasn't good enough for you.

Thank you for the one night stand that we had that made me cry

after, because I knew I was never going to hear from you again.

Thank you for playing with my head.

Thank you for telling me things that were never going to be true.

Thank you for lying to me.

Thank you for being the spitting image of what I perfectly wanted,

only to realizing that it is really just a dream.

Thank you for helping me realize that I deserve, and will have better,

because now I know the signs of what not to look for, when looking

for you.

Thank you.

Tired.

I'm tired of waking up everyday.

To broken promises, non-realistic goals, and people that don't even

care for my soul.

I'm tired of repeating the same cycle of life, Morning, after morning,

night, after night.

I'm tired of just living paycheck to paycheck.

Having to think about doing some evil just to get by.

But I lay my head to sleep at night - knowing I'll wake up and do the

same damn thing over again.

Four Seasons.

You remind me of the seasons.

Your heart is cold like winter,

but I fell for you like the leaves falling during the Fall,

but that quickly changed when you kept me crying tears like rain

during Spring,

but I'll never forget how big your smile was when you walked in the

room, bright like the sun in Summer

but you never stayed around a full year.

 Do You Remember?

Do you remember the last time I looked at you?

My eyes filed with rage, battling against the lies you told me.

Do you remember what you said to me?

The pain written deep against my forehead, as the message plays over

again.

Over and over

Like a broken record that can't stop.

Do you remember why we never spoke again?

Because I couldn't dare listen to your voice or see your face again.

You're happy, I'm happy.

So why replay the tape that'll tear us apart again?

Do You Remember 2.

Do you still remember my birthday?

Do you still remember how I smelled in the morning?

Do you still remember the way you used to look at me?

Do you still remember our memories?

Do you still remember my smile?

Do you still remember my laugh?

Do you still remember my tears?

Do you still remember my pain?

Do you still remember what makes me happy?

Do you still remember me?

Breathe.

Breathe.

Everything is going to be alright.

Your heart might still be cold,

But it can't stay frozen forever.

Lies.

He said he loved you.

He said he wouldn't hurt you.

He said he wanted you.

But he only said these things for you to hear.

Reminded.

I'm reminded of you everyday.

Through pictures.

Memories.

First experiences.

It's like every time I try and get away from you

I'm reminded about the moments we shared.

I'm reminded by the memories that made us laugh.

I'm reminded by the amounts that used to make us cry.

I'm reminded by the pain you shared.

I'm reminded by the mistakes that I used to make.

I'm reminded by the fights that happened often between us.

I'm reminded that I'll never be able to erase you out my head.

Withdrawn.

You became withdrawn from us.

You become withdrawn from my smile.

You became withdrawn from my lips.

You became withdrawn from the memories that we shared.

You become withdrawn to my attraction.

I became withdrawn with the thought of you.

I became withdrawn with being honest.

I became withdrawn with seeing you.

I became withdrawn with coming home at night.

I became withdrawn with you.

And then, it ended.

Empty.

What's an apology without change?

Empty words.

Photographs On The Wall.

I still think back to those days that we took all those pictures

together.

The ones where you held the camera arms length and I smiled at how

you looked at me.

I still look at every photo with a moment that one day you'll come

back to life again.

That the same smile in the photo will become reality, rather than just

a photograph.

I miss the way your eyes squint as your smile lit up the photo and was

the reason I fell in love with you.

That one moment on earth that was so perfect, that we created a

photograph to remember it forever.

That one moment, that I stare at it and smile.

If only I could go back in time,

For one last photo.

Stare.

I stared into your eyes tonight.

I saw the dark shadows of what used to be the past looking into my soul.

I saw the old you.

The you that I fell in love with

The you that nobody ever got to see.

As you stared at me, you went blank.

Almost like you had died and became frozen,

I touched you, and felt nothing.

As I look at you one last time.

I see the same stare

The stare I fell in love with.

And the stare that left me frozen

I'd do anything to feel frozen again

If it meant for you to never walk away from me.

Are You Okay?

Sometimes I ask about you,

It keeps me from having to think about you at night.

Twisted Pictures.

I paint my body

In images of myself

To impress people like you

Only to realize

It's the version of what you want me to be.

You stay intrigued until I wash the paint away.

And then leave when the real me is what you see today.

Belated Birthday.

It's your birthday this week.

As you grow another year, you grow another thorn.

Another thorn, to injure the next person that puts than hands on

you.

Ouch! As they start to suck the small blood that has fallen from their

finger.

Only to realize, all they wanted was just a taste of what you truly had

to offer.

Me > You.

I was given the power to choose.

My life or yours?

At first it would've been so hard,

Now you've made it so easy.

Melody.

Sometimes I listen to songs that remind me of you.

I sing the chorus close to my heart to try and remember that last

moment that we had together.

I listen to the bridge, over, and over, to the thought of you and hope

that maybe I can hear you singing the same song too.

Game. Set. Match.

I feel like I'm losing the game.

I'm losing the game to you.

You Leave Me..

You leave me lonely..

To miss you..

To think about you…

To wonder.

You leave me lonely..

To bleed..

To cheat..

To want something that you're not providing.

You leave me lonely..

And I slowly get to thinking..

Is this even something worth fighting for anymore?

Or are we just saving each other from the heartbreak?

The Old Response.

I used to get messages from you everyday.

You always checked up on me to make sure I was okay.

I was quickly attached to you.

I wanted to talk to you.

I wanted to be in front of you.

I wanted to kiss you.

Until you slowly started fading away,

Your messages stopped coming in.

And then I slowly died.

My heart had burst.

The tears had slowly started rolling down my face.

Until I realize it was meant for you to leave.

Because you wouldn't have been worth it - even if you stayed.

Concrete Scars.

My knees slowly fell along the concrete.

Slowly bleeding out..

I'm alone.

You dropped me.

And walked away without even picking me back up again.

Broken Ankles.

My knees go weak every time I stand next to you,

hoping that one day I collapse

and you slowly pick up

my body, kiss me, and bring me back to life again.

Just A Dream.

You are a dream now.

A washed up memory that occurs when I'm sleeping.

Not a nightmare, but a dream,

A dream of what could've been.

But I wake up everyday to reality,

The chapter without you.

That is why you will always stay a dream, because I deserved to live

life without you.

Our Little Secret.

I'll miss the secrets that we both only know.

Painful Thoughts.

You ever listen to yourself when you talk?

Do you hear the things that come out of your mouth?

How does it feel saying those things to yourself?

It doesn't feel good, does it?

Cigarettes.

I'd rather chew on washed up cigarettes, then to have the same pain I

had when you were here.

Band-Aid.

Can someone come and clear up my scars?

Take the battle bounds off me?

Fill them with love and happiness?

To where they never show again?

 Stolen.

I feel stolen.

Like you took my body and placed it up for sale.

I was sold false dreams of love, only to be bought for display

purposes.

Changing Places.

Never did I think the pain would have changed you.

Changed you into the perfect that I can't even look at anymore.

Changed you to the point where we don't even speak.

Changed you into hating me.

Changed you into living a new life.

The pain wasn't worth it.

Because most importantly, I lost you.

Wounded.

You shot away my happiness,

My heart is bleeding cold,

My smile is drifting into Heaven,

Can you live with this?

Was I Good?

Was I good for you?

Or was I only good in the moment?

Introduced.

I was introduced into your world.

I was introduced to your lifestyle.

I was introduced to so much of you, that I became a version of you.

I was introduced to new ideas.

I was introduced to new aspirations.

I was so introduced to you, I had lost myself.

 The Last Conversation.

It's been some months since we have last spoke.

I haven't seen you, you haven't seen me.

But some days I do wish we could meet face to face

just so I can make sure everything with you is okay.

Purity.

II.

The New Attraction.

Do you chase the same people you attract?

What ever happened to opposites being sexy?

Why is it we go for what we are interested in, instead of what is going to change the usual attraction of what we're accustomed too?

Closure We All Wished For.

We all want closure, but we're all afraid of reaching out to that person

to have the closure we all desire.

Bittersweet.

I'm bitter.

Absolutely.

I have every right to be.

Do you know why?

Because now I have pain from you

that'll never heal.

You don't understand that.

You never will.

I gave my heart to a fool

And now I'm only left with battle scars.

The Closure.

You are a strong person, you did it, you left.

- be happy.

Standards.

Do you meet the standards of today's love market?

Do you look like the person you see on TV?

Do you have a nice job?

What goals do you have going for yourself?

Do you seek validation in others?

Are you pretty enough?

Are you in school?

Why do we have

So many standards

That we try to seek in a person,

that we overlook the qualities that matter most?

Because standards are what now matter.

Standards are the new norm.

Standards are what you have to have in order to live a "successful"
life

Fuck the standards.

Change the standards.

Embrace YOUR standards.

Note To Self.

I feel good.

I look good.

I am good.

I deserve good.

I taste good.

I will always be good.

- my inner self

Approval.

I scroll down the pictures of the people I aspire to be. Only to realize, is this their reality, or the false image of what they want me to see?

Fix yourself.

Stop trying to fit in with the aspirations of what you see on TV.

Stop comparing yourself to the models on Instagram whose filters
are only a reality of what you actually

don't see.

Stop crying about these foolish individuals that don't deserve you,
but only want to crave how you feel on

the inside.

Stop trying to control every aspect of your life that you're
overlooking the beauty of what you're living in

right now.

Stop trying to accomplish things, that are beyond your reach right
now.

Stop trying to grow past your age, because someone is doing better
than you.

Stop.

After Hours.

Why is it that your mind relaxes at 12am?

That you think more about your heart than you do in the other hours

of the day?

Why is it that you wonder about your past, the relationships that

didn't work, the old life you used to live,

The growth of who you have become?

Why is it that when the clock strikes at 12? You become a new

person?

Rewind The Past.

What happens to your past relationships?

Do they fade away or do they still haunt you at night?

Do you still think about them in certain moments of the day?

Do you wish things didn't happen the way they did?

Do you reach out to them?

Do you apologize?

Do you still love them?

Do the feelings fade away?

Is what is now over, still ever not thought about?

Single.

Being single is fun they said.

Being single is about you they said.

Being single is free they said.

Being single is happy they said.

But what they didn't tell you..

Being single hurts.

Being single is lonely.

Being single causes you to overthink.

Being single makes you insecure.

But what you'll learn..

Being single is about you.

Being single is independent.

Being single is about learning.

Being single is about growing.

Being single is about looking into your past mistakes.

Being single is about living.

Being single is about YOU.

Hijack.

Hijack my heart and take it to places that it has never been.

What Is This?

Where am I?

Is this the Earth that I was born into?

Is this how life really is?

Is this the human distraction that I'm supposed to endure on to keep
my mind from wondering into places

that are not meant to me?

Why is this even real?

Who is real?

Why is it so hard to love someone that doesn't love back?

Why are humans different from one another?

If there is so many people in this world, why are we all searching for
the one thing that was created in order

for life to continue?

Why?

Mind Games.

Did you come into my life to play with my mind?

Did you twist my thoughts to keep me from seeking admiration from another person?

Were you being selfish?

What were you thinking?

Opening up to you every single day,

Putting you before others,

Re-cutting these wounds that were closed for years.

To open the same scar that I spent years closing.

What were you thinking?

To use me.

To fill my head up with words.

To kiss me.

To use my body as a toy.

What were you thinking?

Did you ever think about how I would feel when you left?

Did you ever continue to think about me after it was over?

What were you thinking?

Did you win a prize?

To play with my mind.

Hope this game was worth the battle at the end.

Questions For You..

Can I be the number that you call late at night?

The number when you want someone to hold?

The number when you want someone to talk too?

The number when you need a shoulder to lean on?

The number when you're having a bad day?

Can I be?

The sparkle in your eye?

The grin to your smile?

The reason why you wake up everyday?

Can I Be?

The one?

That one?

Your one?

Can I?

.... Please?

Curious about who you are.

Curious about your past.

Curious about what you want to do with my body.

Curious about your darkest secrets.

Let's explore the curious side of me & you.

I talk to myself often to keep myself entertained.

I feel like I'm my own best friend.

I don't trust anyone anymore.

I don't listen to anyone anymore.

It's me against the world.

And I'm completely fine with that, I don't need any new friends. I need new goals.

"Unknown Album."

I could write a whole album about you.

Just so you can listen to all the thoughts I think about.

Repeated Cycle <.

Why is it when you meet someone new,

They always have the same intentions as the last person you

previously met?

The End Goal.

We run through others to get closer to the one that we're supposed

to spend the rest of our life with.

Church For The Mind.

Get away from the computer.

Get outside the house.

Get creative.

Attend an event.

Network.

Don't give up.

Keep trying.

Bo$$ UP.

Life is about being your own boss.

Take control of your life.

Cleanse your body and mind.

Learn more about yourself.

Pace.

Evaluating your life does nothing for your sanity.

YOUR pace is okay.

The New Sunday.

Less TV and more podcasts.

Financial You.

If you don't take care of yourself, the money won't come.

Instagram 2.0

When you wipe the labels away, what else do you have to bring to the

table?

Don't be the person that dressed their whole life trying to impress

others - only to realize everything you did was just for a photo.

Forgive.

Don't put pity on your ex, wish for them the love that you weren't

able to provide them.

Wish for them to have a better life, wish for them to be happy

- that's love.

Keep yourself on a pedestal,

Know that everyone doesn't deserve you

And you don't need to mix everyone's energy with yours.

Pressure.

III.

Love Is Like The Movies.

The pressure to this lifestyle is always something that is so different. I always believe my life will be like a movie. Someone is going to walk into my life, make me smile, fight through the hard times with me. Then when I'm ready to give up, they beg for another chance. You'll kiss me so hard that I'll know you want me forever. This isn't how love works, I know that. But who says I can't have my perfect story? If my life was a movie, then I would probably want to never finish it to the end.

Magical Dates.

We go on magical dates.

We find the smallest memory of the simplest thing as going out to

eat, so romantic, that we want this to

happen, over, and over, again.

We love the idea of someone looking into our eyes while we're

expressing ourselves, that we feel like they

are staring into our soul.

We feel like they can see every negative emotion that we choose not

to express in our initial date.

Our magical dates appear to be so magical, that the second they turn

bad - we realize that we are back to reality again.

#RelationshipGoals.

You want it.

The attention.

Everyone to see how happy you are.

How you've accomplished that "perfect love story"

You want the hashtags.

You want everyone to know, "oh that's so and so."

You want to be dreamed of.

You want to be known.

Heart < Head.

We always believe every person that comes along is the right one.

But my heart has led me in the wrong

direction so many times, that I don't even know who to trust.

Me.

I'm very emotional.

I'm not going to ever change that.

I'm not going to apologize for that.

I'm a hopeless romantic in a hook-up culture.

But one day, I'll find the right person that will play sad songs in the

rain to make me smile, and I'll realize

this was all worth it.

Modern Relationship.

We don't meet up anymore.

We don't go on dates.

The modern relationship is so complex, that the simplest tasks to achieve in getting to know someone is the

hardest thing that we are asking for.

We lack the levels of consistency.

We decide that we "like" each other until the "like" goes away.

We use general excuses to not talk to one another because we don't want to rush commitment, but we also

want to do our own thing.

We want to have our cake and eat it too. We dream of the attention that we desire, but lack the effort in

giving to another person in order to receive the same thing back.

We find love with a swipe right, or with an "unlocked" pic, that we forget to ask ourselves, is this how we

want to tell our future generation how we met?

Do you wanna end the old cycle of actually getting to know a person?

Marriage.

You have this pressure that getting married is a priority. You feel like

that is the only thing stopping you from

living a healthy and happy life. You want the foundation of building

with another person and creating a life

to share with them.

But you are still so young.

Busy Body.

We keep ourselves busy.

To hide the distraction that we're addicted to love.

The Watchers.

We choose to seek validation from people that are only wanting to

watch our lives from the outside.

The Interview.

Hi?

What's your name?

What are your dreams?

Why do you like me?

Do I intrigued you?

What makes you different?

What's something bad about you?

This has now become the new questionnaire when it comes to dating.

We don't date to date anymore, we date to seek validation as if the other party is trying out for a job interview. The job interview to my heart, are you qualified for the position? Are you going to take it serious? The pay is spending the rest of your life with me, are you ready for that?

What We Do.

As a hopeless romantic, we have this challenging time trying to juggle with loving someone else and hope for our true love, or if were supposed to love ourselves and just be happy with being independent.

We don't want that, we thrive off someone else's positive energy, we thrive off the consistency of someone wanting to learn more about us everyday.

Why would we want to trade that in to learn more about ourselves, only to fall asleep to nothing at night?

Word Of Advice.

"Stop looking for love, let it come to you."

- They said.

My reaction:

"I'm always fucking looking. Even when I'm not supposed too, I still

have the thought in my head of looking."

And when i saw you.

Have you ever had the thought of looking into someone's eyes and

seeing that you could spend the rest of your life with them?

Distraction.

I want you to be a distraction.

Make me forget my regular day and take my mind out of reality for just a moment.

Distract me from the truth, so I can figure out what's real.

Distract me from the comfort of being comfortable to where I get nervous around you.

Distract me from all my problems to where I never have to experience them again.

Can you be my distraction?

The Broken Puzzle.

We have this problem,

We want you to think about us.

We want you to think about us as much that you can't go a second
without wondering how our day is

going.

We want you to be obsessive.

In a good way.

We want to be the puzzle that if you lose one piece, you can't put the
puzzle together anymore.

Think about me.

Think about us.

Think about the future.

With me.

Doesn't that sound like a life worth living?

Flowers > Lottery.

The thoughts of flowers from you makes me more excited than

winning the lottery.

Wishful Dreaming.

Awww seems to make you smile more in a text message.

A good morning text seems to light up your day and start It on a new adventure.

A random FaceTime call makes you feel like a little kid again.

You wake up to use the restroom from sleeping and have a long paragraph text message about how they feel

about you.

Those are the things you wish for.

The Advice Column.

Your friends come to you for advice, knowing you give them the best

advice you can't even give yourself.

Impractical.

Some days I think that love is impractical.

I believe that our generation has lost it all.

Lost the emotion of falling in love with someone else.

Pregnancy has become the new lifetime commitment with having
someone for the rest of your life but no

relationship.

It's now impractical to have a "Real" first date anymore.

Impractical to think I could even fall in love with you now.

Impractical to believe that you'll miss me when I leave.

Impractical to fight when things get hard, because you can go on
social media and find your next one.

Impractical to even try anymore.

Our generation has lost the foundation of love.

Commitment is longer than 72 days.

Impractical for me to believe love is even real anymore.

Impractical to think love is now just in the movies.

The Dream One.

As hopeless romantics, we have the feeling that we are so stuck on

finding the perfect qualities in a person,

that we feel like we will never find our perfect match.

We find imperfections in everyone, the smallest things about a person

can makes us lose interest in them

very quickly.

We strive for the person we're interested in to have committed goals

and want more out of what life has to offer.

If we continue to continue the same thinking cycle, will we ever find

the perfect one?

Or is it too perfect to even become?

Commitment.

Commitment is so damn romantic.

Matchmaker.

Why is it the ones that we want never want us, and the ones that we don't want, are the sweetest?

Gaze With The Stars.

Can we sit and talk about our days together? In the back of the truck

with the stars outside?

Adventurous.

Let's be adventurous.

Let's do things we've never done before.

Let's experience life together.

Let's travel the world.

Let's kiss each other.

Let's fall in love.

All over again.

Tender.

Your soul is so tender

That I'm afraid to touch it.

Love is so blind, that sometimes, I wonder if I'm even good enough

to open my eyes.

Ever.last

We all want that everlasting love.

But aren't willing to put in the work to make it ever-last.

You.

All you can do is take one day at a time.

Learn from your mistakes and become a better person day by day.

You can't erase the past, but you can change your future.

You can love someone new, you can still be the hopeless romantic
you know your heart wants.

You can still kiss the person of your dreams.

You can still hold their hand.

You can still be you.

Dedication:

This book is dedicated to those that might have thought they were never going to find love again. I want you all to know that you are not alone, I'm a-lot like you. I'm a man that is in love with the idea of love, and that love will come for you. Love is everywhere. I want you to know to not give up. To use your thoughts as a stepping stool to find the person that you are meant to be with. Challenge yourself, know what you are worth and don't ever stop being the hopeless romantic that is currently lost in a hookup culture.

Follow the Author:

Instagram: @storyofdvonte

Twitter: @VonteKnowsItAll

andwhenikissedyou.

Made in the USA
Middletown, DE
30 July 2022

70231535R00060